A TRUE BOOK

Ecology
The Study of Ecosystems

SUSAN H. GRAY

Children's Press®
An Imprint of Scholastic Inc.
New York Toronto London Auckland Sydney
Mexico City New Delhi Hong Kong
Danbury, Connecticut

Content Consultant
Dr. Laura Burkle
Assistant Professor of Ecology
Montana State University
Bozeman, Montana

Library of Congress Cataloging-in-Publication Data

Gray, Susan Heinrichs.
  Ecology the study of ecosystems/by Susan H. Gray.
      p. cm.—(A true book)
  Includes bibliographical references and index.
  ISBN-13: 978-0-531-24675-7 (lib. bdg.)   ISBN-10: 0-531-24675-2 (lib. bdg.)
  ISBN-13: 978-0-531-28269-4 (pbk.)   ISBN-10: 0-531-28269-4 (pbk.)
  1. Ecology—Juvenile literature. I. Title. II. Series.
  QH541.14.G648 2012
  577—dc23   2011030963

All rights reserved. Published in 2012 by Children's Press, an imprint of Scholastic Inc.
Printed in China 62
SCHOLASTIC, CHILDREN'S PRESS, A TRUE BOOK, and associated logos are trademarks and/or registered trademarks of Scholastic Inc.
5 6 7 8 9 10 R 21 20 19 18 17 16 15

Find the Truth!

Everything you are about to read is true *except* for one of the sentences on this page.

Which one is **TRUE**?

T or F An ecologist's main job is to get people to recycle.

T or F Ecosystems include nonliving things such as rocks.

Find the answers in this book.

Contents

THE **BIG** TRUTH!

A View of the Rain Forest

4

Some animals hunt others for food.

The shape of the
land is one element
of ecology.

Ecologists study
natural environments
all around the world.

CHAPTER 1

The ABCs of Ecology

In Colorado, a young woman explains to campers why ticks are common in the area. In Florida, a college student checks on some newly hatched fish. In Texas, a lab worker is creating a new method to keep swimming pools clean. On the island of Guam, a scientist figures out the best way to keep snakes from taking over the food chain. What do these people have in common? They are all ecologists.

This rainforest plant depends on the ant communities that grow on it to survive.

Biotic and Abiotic

Ecology is the study of the relationships between living organisms and their **environments**. Every environment is made up of living and nonliving things. For example, living things in a hawk's environment might include snakes, ferrets, pine trees, and poison ivy. Ecologists call them **biotic** factors. The nonliving things might be clean air, sunlight, a mountain, a rocky stream, and cold temperatures at night. Ecologists say these are **abiotic** factors.

Abiotic and biotic factors work together in every natural environment.

Abiotic, biotic, cycles, and change are sometimes called the ABCs of ecology.

Many large birds hunt and eat smaller animals such as fish.

Cycles

Ecologists study how these factors interact in cycles. A cycle is a series of events that keeps repeating. One example is the seasons. As seasons change, abiotic factors change. Winter provides less sunlight than summer. Biotic factors must also change. Animals might sleep through the winter when there is less sunlight and warmth. The food chain is another cycle. Nutrients are passed from one living thing to another as organisms eat and are eaten.

Change

Ecologists also study how organisms are affected by changes in the environment. They might ask how a hawk would respond if a new kind of snake came into the environment. They may wonder how a dam on a rocky stream would affect the hawk. They try to get the best understanding of the hawk's ecology. Then they can predict what will happen when the hawk's environment changes.

Ecologists attach tags to animals that allow them to identify the same animals later.

Laws now limit the chemicals in detergents.

Water samples allow ecologists to test for harmful substances.

Putting It Into Action

In the 1960s, **algae** had taken over many lakes. Fish were dying. Ecologists learned that cities were dumping wastewater into those lakes. It included soapy water from washing machines. The soap contained nutrients that helped algae multiply. As algae died, tiny organisms ate them. This used up oxygen. Fish suffocated and died.

The solution to this problem involved water, chemistry, plants, and animals. Ecologists were the perfect people to find what went wrong and how to fix it.

Ancient Egyptians did not think of themselves as ecologists, but they understood how to make plants grow.

CHAPTER 2

Ecology in History

The roots of ecology go back thousands of years. Farmers in ancient times noticed that plants grew better when they had good soil and enough rain. Early hunters knew which environments had buffalo or mammoths. But around 2,300 years ago, a Greek thinker named Theophrastus began to put things together. Theophrastus examined sprouting seeds and young plants. He wrote of the abiotic factors that affected plant growth.

"Ecology" comes from the Greek word *oikos* meaning "household" or "home."

Ecology Moves Forward

For many years, scientists were more interested in individual **species**. They didn't pay attention to species' environments. But in the 1700s, Carl Linnaeus began looking at how animals were related. He also studied how different animals shared an environment. He noticed that the

animals stayed in balance. Each species had enough to eat. Each also had a large enough population to survive if members were eaten by other species.

Carl Linnaeus was one of the earliest ecologists.

Alexander von Humboldt's studies in Central and South America were a major influence on later ecologists.

In 1799, a young scientist named Alexander von Humboldt studied the plants and animals of Central and South America. He saw that certain types of plants always seemed to appear together. He also noticed how abiotic factors affected those plants. In the 1800s, Charles Darwin built on Humboldt's ideas. In the Galápagos Islands, Darwin saw how plants and animals depended on each other to survive.

In the 20th century, ecologists began to demonstrate how important it was to understand how biotic and abiotic factors interact. In the 1930s, American ecologist Paul Sears saw that cattle were damaging grasslands. Poor farming methods were also ruining the soil. Sears wrote a book called *Deserts on the March* that explained the problem to the public.

Earth Day is celebrated in more than 175 countries each year on April 22.

Ecology Timeline

330 BCE
Theophrastus studies seeds and plant growth.

1760
Linnaeus writes that nature stays in balance.

In the 1960s, scientist Rachel Carson wrote about pollution. Her book, *Silent Spring*, helped make people aware of the dangers of insect spray. Widespread use damaged the water, air, and soil. This could lead to health problems and damage food supplies. Soon, new laws were passed in the United States to better protect the environment from pollution.

1799–1804
Humboldt studies the plants of Central and South America.

1935
Sears writes *Deserts on the March.*

1963
President Lyndon Johnson signs the first Clean Air Act.

Ecologists study how plants and animals interact with each other.

CHAPTER 3

Ecosystems

Ecologists like to "think big." Most ecologists do not just study the life of a mouse or learn where ferns grow best. Instead, they want to know which animals eat the mouse. They wonder if the mouse hides under those ferns or if it eats crickets that hide there. They want to know what the crickets eat. Some ecologists want to understand the whole **community** in a certain area.

The plant community here includes trees, grasses, and shrubs.

What Is an Ecosystem?

An ecosystem incudes an area's biotic factors—its plant and animal communities. It also includes the area's abiotic factors. In an ecosystem, every plant and animal has a job to do. They work together in a cycle. In a lake ecosystem, algae produce oxygen. Tiny floating organisms eat algae and also breathe the oxygen. These organisms become food for fish. Fish produce carbon dioxide when they breathe. The algae use carbon dioxide to live and grow.

Underwater ecosystems are much different from those on land.

A well-stocked aquarium is a homemade ecosystem.

Prairie ecosystems are home to many different species of animals and wild grasses.

An ecosystem might be as small as a pond. It might be as large as a rain forest. Other ecosystems are prairies, swamps, coral reefs, and the woods behind a house. No ecosystem is closed off from the rest of the world. Sunlight comes in from the outside. Animals enter and leave. Birds carry off plant seeds. Rain washes insects into other nearby ecosystems. Water drops in as rain and washes out with a river.

Food Chains

When ecologists look at ecosystems, they often want to understand its food chains. The food chain is simply who eats what in the system. Plants are first in the food chain. They take in energy from sunlight. They use it to change chemicals in their cells into sugar. The sugar helps them live and grow. Plants are first in the chain because they use the sun to produce food instead of eating other organisms.

Plants get important nutrients from the sunlight and the soil.

Animals that eat only plants are called herbivores.

Rabbits eat a variety of flowers and grasses.

Plant-eating animals are next. These include grasshoppers, rabbits, and buffalo. **Predators** that eat them are the next link. Mice eat grasshoppers. Wolves eat rabbits and buffalo. Some predators, such as wolves, hawks, and boa constrictors, are at the top of the food chain. Other animals do not kill them for food. But when they die, tiny organisms help decompose their bodies. This adds nutrients to the soil, which helps nourish plants. The cycle begins again.

Food Webs

In nature, food chains can become very complex. An animal may be a predator one day but become **prey** the next day. For example, a mouse eats a grasshopper. But then the mouse itself becomes food for an eagle. A food chain cannot show all of the feeding patterns in an ecosystem. Instead, ecologists use a food web. It is actually many food chains woven together.

The ocean's food web includes plants and animals of all sizes.

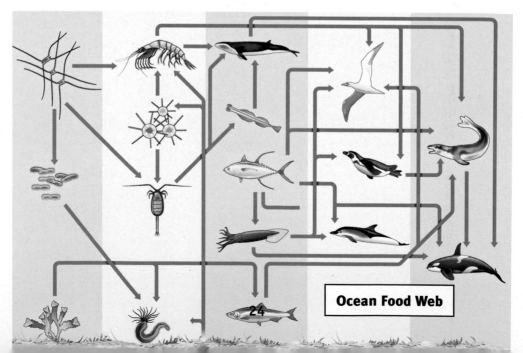

Ocean Food Web

24

Learning to Plan Ahead

Beetles and other insects often attack sugarcane. To protect their crops, Australia's Bureau of Sugar Experiment Stations did something drastic. They brought in cane toads from another country to eat the pests. Soon, the bureau realized its mistake. The toads began eating other animals. The poison in the toad's skin killed people's pets. The toads became the new pests.

Cane toads can live more than 15 years in captivity!

Different Ecosystems

Every ecosystem is important. But one that has gained much attention is the Amazon rain forest. This ecosystem is enormous. It covers much of South America. Millions of kinds of plants and animals live there. Many are found nowhere else in the world. And scientists discover new ones every year. The rain forest is important for another reason. Its trees produce around 20 percent of the world's oxygen.

Most of the Amazon rain forest is in Brazil.

Scientists work hard to protect rain forest ecosystems from disappearing.

Many fish live among the roots and grasses of estuaries.

An **estuary** is also an important ecosystem. An estuary is a wetland where a river meets the ocean. Grasses and trees often grow in the marshes nearby. Some people might call it a wasteland and say it is useless. But ecologists have found that young fish find protection here. They have also found that the mesh of grasses and roots can serve as a filter. They keep **pollutants** from reaching the ocean.

Deer, acorns, and ticks all share the same ecosystem.

An oak forest is a woodland ecosystem. In a dense forest, little sunlight reaches the ground. Grass is patchy. Leaves and acorns cover the ground instead. Deer feed on the acorns. Ticks then feed on the deer. Ecologists have studied this ecosystem. They see that where acorns are plentiful, deer and ticks are, too. Ticks carry a disease called Lyme disease. Ecologists warn campers that they have higher chances of getting Lyme disease in areas covered in acorns.

Coral reefs are structures built by tiny ocean animals. The coral animals build hard cups to live in. As their colony grows, the animals build new cups on top of old ones. Eventually, the animals might create a very large reef. As it grows, more and more animals come to live there. Tiny fish find safety in its cracks and spaces. Sea stars and crabs creep about, finding food.

The world's largest reef system is Australia's Great Barrier Reef.

Coral is often bright and colorful, with interesting shapes.

A View of the Rain Forest

Rain forests have four layers: the emergent layer, the canopy, the understory, and the forest floor. Each includes countless organisms that keep the forest healthy. Many of these organisms are in danger.

The emergent layer has the tallest trees. Trees provide homes for most rain forest creatures. They also provide products such as rubber and wood to humans. Deforestation by farmers and loggers destroys several million acres of trees each year.

Most species live around the dense canopy. Orangutans are one example. They live only in Indonesia. As deforestation continues, the orangutans' home shrinks. Their numbers are decreasing quickly.

The understory includes many different plants. Rain forest plants are often used in medicine, including many cancer treatments. But these plants are disappearing with the forest's trees.

Compared to the layers above, few plants and animals live on the forest floor. But native peoples have made it their home for centuries. Outsiders and deforestation drive many native people out. Entire cultures can be lost this way. So can generations of rain forest knowledge.

When people are careless, they damage the ecosystem.

CHAPTER 4

Protecting the Ecosystems

Ecology is the study of the links between plants and animals. Ecologists try to see how entire ecosystems work. They understand the connections between living and nonliving things. They know that it is important to protect these things. So ecologists believe in **conservation**. To conserve is to prevent the harm, waste, or destruction of living and nonliving things. Conservation is important not only to ecologists. It is important to everyone.

 Scientists have found plastic scraps in the stomachs of fish.

Reduce, Reuse, and Recycle

There are many things that people can do to conserve ecosystems. For instance, they can reduce the amount of materials they use. They can avoid using juice boxes and bottled water. Instead, they can fill their own bottles with juice or tap water. People might also turn off the water while they brush their teeth.

A faucet dripping once every second wastes 86,400 drops of water a day.

Use your own water bottles to avoid creating trash.

Thrift stores are great places to shop for used clothing.

Reusing items is another way to conserve resources. Students often do this by using both sides of their printer paper. Some kids buy used computer games and DVDs online or at local stores. Many teens love to shop at used clothing stores. Homeowners can use the leaves that fall in autumn and grass clippings left over from mowing the lawn. They can spread them on gardens to make the soil healthier.

Some community festivals have special recycling booths. Visitors are encouraged to recycle utensils, bottles, and other items.

Most people know that they can recycle glass, paper, aluminum cans, and plastic bottles. But some recycling centers accept many other things. Some will buy aluminum pots and pans. Others buy the copper from old air conditioners and small motors. Many schools recycle printer cartridges and cell phones to raise money. And some organizations take old bicycles, fix them up, and give them away.

Thinking First

Many years ago, people did not understand ecosystems. They built highways and expanded cities, but did not consider the harm they might be doing. Today, ecologists come in before large building projects are started. They study the landforms and the water flow in the area. They look at the plants and animals that will be affected. Sometimes they suggest better places to build, where the projects will not harm the ecosystem.

Ecologists keep a close eye on tundra ecosystems, where temperatures are rising and large amounts of ice are melting.

CHAPTER 5

Ecologists at Work Today

Ecosystems change through time. Ecologists study these changes to determine what is causing them. Sometimes new species are added to the ecosystem. Sometimes weather patterns change. Ecologists figure out whether these changes are damaging the ecosystem. If they are, the scientists find ways to stop the damage. Other ecologists keep track of the changes. They try to determine how ecosystems will continue to change in the future.

Tundras are cold, dry regions with short, stumpy grass.

Solving Today's Problems

Some ecologists are studying plant and animal invaders. These are species that have moved into areas where they do not belong. The cane toad is one example. Another is the **kudzu** plant in the United States. Kudzu was brought in from Japan to feed farm animals. But it quickly grew out of control. It destroys ecosystems by smothering other plants. Now ecologists are searching for the best way to manage it.

Kudzu contains a chemical that relieves headaches.

Kudzu can quickly overtake the other plants around it.

40

Sea otters help keep sea urchin populations in check.

Some ecologists notice food chain problems. In Africa, a disease killed many wildebeest. These large plant eaters keep shrubs under control. When wildebeest numbers shrank, more shrubs grew and many wildfires broke out.

Elsewhere, sea otters were disappearing along some coastlines. The otters eat sea urchins. The sea urchins eat **kelp**. When the otters disappeared, sea urchins began destroying the kelp forests. Ecologists study these problems and determine what can be done to help.

The number of ecology jobs is expected to grow in the future.

Many universities offer programs in ecology.

Ecologists are spotting problems in the environment before anyone else. They are finding ways to protect endangered animals. Some ecologists are stopping the spread of harmful organisms. Others are showing farmers better ways to grow and protect their crops. Still others are teaching classes or helping people understand the importance of conservation. All ecologists are working to save the earth and its ecosystems. ★

True Statistics

Amount of energy used to make aluminum cans from recycled material: About 95 percent less than when cans are made from new materials

State with the highest percentage of forest land: Maine, with almost 90 percent of the state listed as wooded area

Number of plastic bottles used in America: About 2.5 million bottles every hour

Amount of leaves and grass clippings thrown away in America: About 24 million tons (22 metric tons) every year

Number of fish species living on and around the Great Barrier Reef: More than 1,500

Average size of an adult cane toad: 2.9 lb. (1.3 kg)

Did you find the truth?

F An ecologist's main job is to get people to recycle.

T Ecosystems include nonliving things such as rocks.

Resources

Books

Berkenkamp, Lauri. *Discover the Oceans: The World's Largest Ecosystem*. White River Junction, VT: Nomad Press, 2009.

Davis, Barbara J. *Biomes and Ecosystems*. New York: Gareth Stevens Publishing, 2007.

Delannoy, Isabelle. *Our Living Earth: A Story of People, Ecology, and Preservation*. New York: Abrams Books for Young Readers, 2008.

Kelsey, Elin. *Not Your Typical Book About the Environment*. Toronto, ON: Owlkids Books, 2010.

Moore, Heidi. *Ocean Food Chains*. Chicago: Heinemann-Raintree, 2010.

Rohmer, Harriet. *Heroes of the Environment: True Stories of People Who Are Helping to Protect Our Planet*. San Francisco: Chronicle Books, 2009.

Silverman, Buffy. *Desert Food Chains*. Chicago: Heinemann-Raintree, 2010.

Venezia, Mike. *Rachel Carson*. New York: Children's Press, 2010.

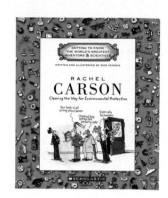

Organizations and Web Sites

Kids Do Ecology
http://kids.nceas.ucsb.edu
Visitors to this site can learn what ecologists do, read about the earth's ecological communities, and pick up some ideas for classroom projects.

Kids.gov—Science: Our Planet
www.kids.gov/k_5/k_5_science_earth.shtml
This site has links to pages covering the environment, different ecosystems, ways to protect the planet, and much more.

Places to Visit

Arizona-Sonora Desert Museum
2021 North Kinney Road
Tucson, Arizona 85743
(520) 883-2702
www.desertmuseum.org
Visit the exhibits on cactus, desert grasslands, and desert gardens to learn about the desert ecosystem.

Monterey Bay Aquarium
886 Cannery Row
Monterey, CA 93940
(831) 648-4800
www.montereybayaquarium.org
Visit the kelp forest, sea otters, and other inhabitants of underwater ecosystems.

Visit this Scholastic web site for more information on ecology:
www.factsfornow.scholastic.com

Important Words

abiotic (ay-bye-AH-tik) — having to do with nonliving things

algae (AL-jee) — small plants without roots or stems that grow mainly in water

biotic (bye-AH-tik) — having to do with living things

community (kuh-MYOO-ni-tee) — a group of living things that lives in one place and interact

conservation (kahn-sur-VAY-shuhn) — the protection of valuable things

environments (en-VYE-ruhn-muhnts) — the natural surroundings of living things

estuary (ES-choo-er-ee) — the wide part of a river, where it joins the ocean

kelp (KELP) — a large, edible, brown seaweed

kudzu (KUD-zoo) — a fast-growing Asian vine

pollutants (puh-LOO-tuhnts) — substances that contaminate another substance

predators (PREH-duh-turz) — animals that live by hunting other animals for food

prey (PRAY) — an animal hunted by another animal for food

species (SPEE-sheez) — one of the groups into which animals and plants are divided

Index

Page numbers in **bold** indicate illustrations

About the Author

Susan H. Gray has a master's degree in zoology and has also studied geology and paleontology. She has written more than 120 reference books for children. Susan especially likes to write on topics that engage children in science. She and her husband, Michael, live in Cabot, Arkansas.